AF596514
Author' Anita Johnson-Brown

Anita Brown's Commentary

All About Love

Anita Brown's Commentary was written and created by
Anita Johnson-Brown

Anita Brown's Commentary—Anita Brown's Commentary is my opinion, about the facts of life and other subjects of matter, and the words written are not meant to persuade how you choose to live. Or think.

About the Author

Legal Wife of Christopher Maurice Brown/Entertainer Chris Brown, I am a mother, Author, Self-Publisher, News Reporter, Photographer, Film Reviewer, and Editor and Owner, of The Los Angeles News.

Author
Anita Johnson-Brown

Welcome to the world of Author Anita Johnson-Brown, enter the realm of my thoughts, desires, and how I depict what I visualize, imagine, and define as reality. My desires run deep, romantically I only have room in my heart for one man, but I love all people, and treat people with the love and respect they deserve.
There is no gift as precious as the gift of LOVE!
Written by Anita Johnson-Brown

Defining Love in Friendship

Friendship Love is a platonic journey of human connections with people who I consider attractive mentally, we jive, vibe, and unite, with the understanding of respecting each other's boundaries, and privacy, sharing special times, having fun, learning from each, welcoming each other's company, being sympathetic and empathetic when the time arises, laughing together, a bit teasing without hurting the other person, and enjoying every moment of building true and great friendships while helping when it's necessary.

You must be special for me to allow you in my life, and although I believe in sisterhood and woman bonding, and never stabbing a female friend in the back or any female for that fact, I am fond of platonic relationships with gentlemen. I find men remarkably interesting, and open with me. I am a woman who can discuss anything without judgment while giving good advice on how to spice up relationships, however, there are some things I will not discuss with male or female friends, and that is the intimate moments I share with the man I love, such as the size of private body parts, and any intimacy issues.

The sayings of Anita Johnson-Brown-Written by Anita Johnson-Brown

True Love is hard to find, just as True friendship.
Deception is in the mind and heart of the deceiver, and the deceiver's act of deception affects not only the victim personally, but it also affects every part of the person's life, so choose your friends and lovers wisely. Guard your Heart but allow yourself to share love, and kindness accordingly.

Written by Anita Johnson-Brown

Trust

To be able to love and trust someone is the most beautiful thing that could happen, to be able to love, and trust the one you LOVE is the ultimate pleasure of love.
Written by Anita Johnson-Brown

Days of Love, Anita Browns Commentary

-
-

Expressions of love are not always intimate when platonic friendships are on the rise, however, gestures of love can be present when intimacy and flirtatious language, is expressed in desires of body language, words spoken, movement of the body, and sentiments of the mind are combined.
If gestures of intimacy are not returned, then the relationship is platonic LOVE.

Written by Anita Johnson-Brown

Days of Love Anita Brown's Commentary: Written by Anita Johnson-Brown

-
-

Days of Love

There's no greater illusion than the one you've created in real life, of the fantasy of perfect love, love comes with strings attached, emotions, and heartfelt sentiments, while you are embodied with denying the perils of temptation, freedom to communicate, and express desires without, holding back what must be said to fulfill, the unbreakable bonds of LOVE.
Communication with the one you love should have no conversational boundaries or anger zones.
Written by Anita Johnson-Brown

Days of Love Anita Brown's Commentary:

-

Celebrating the month of December in the spirit of Love.

Love, at first sight, is a true and meaningful experience, getting to know the one you love takes time, there is no time limit on Cupid's arrow of LOVE.
Loving you Always.
Written by Anita Johnson-Brown

Days of Love Anita Brown's Commentary:

-
-

Sentiments of LOVE can be expressed in many ways; however, the endearing vows of love should not cause another to endure sly undertones of disrepute, emotional anguish, or disrespect.

Written by Anita Johnson-Brown

Anita Brown's Commentary: Where is my Gift?

-
-
-

It is the gift-giving season, the amount of the gift is unimportant, it is the thought that counts. Gifts of sentimental value create the best memories.

Written by Anita Johnson-Brown

Anita Brown's Commentary: Patience

-
-
-
-

Blessings are never blocked; they are delayed for the right moment.

Anita Brown's Commentary: Think about It! One more time.

-
-

-
-

1. Evil penetrates through the bone, and evil-doers seem to get away with deeds of dirt, wrong-doing, defamation, and scandal for an eternity, but they do have their time, and when the justice of good comes calling, it seeks its revenge, in a terminology, known as the circle of the go and come around.
2. Sowing good seeds produces good fruit; however, Things that happen in everyday life events will always be a part of all our lives.
3. Money does not buy love; it buys the love of company.
4. Being alone can cause a feeling of isolation and loneliness but taking time to get to know oneself is the ultimate gift of self-love.

Blooming of Nature
As the leaves fall from the tree in their due season, so does the replenishing of the earth in the blooming forces of nature., just as the balance of living beings on the earth.

Written by Anita Johnson-Brown

Anita Brown's Commentary: Something to think about

-
-
-
-

Self-love is a question of virtue, and in some instances, intimacy is an expression of love, and lust is an inquisitive desire, and a bittersweet temptation.

Please note—Anita Brown's Commentary is my opinion, about the facts of life and other subjects of matter, and the words written are not meant to persuade how you choose to live.
Written by Anita Johnson-Brown

Anita Brown's Commentary: Tell me about it

•

•

•

•

1. When things do not work out the way you planned, God has another path for you to enter, and it is a door no mortal man can close. There will be difficulties, but you will gain knowledge, wisdom understanding, and a learning experience you can teach others.
2. You do not have to be wealthy to be wise, you need to be clever to be wealthy, however, a man should not be judged by his wealth, but by his deeds.
3. Never claim earthy material, with a boasting gesture, while those in poverty suffer, you did not build the earth, you were allowed to build upon it. The forces of Mother Nature that work to maintain a healthy planet can discharge its immunities to balance the earth. (In other words (where we stand can be swept from under our feet at any time)
4. Money is said to be the root of evil, and so is envy and jealousy.
5. Never judge a man or a woman by the attire they wear, but by one's personality and attitude.
6. Anyone who brings you out of character is bad for your soul and mental wellness.
Written by Anita Johnson-Brown

Take a moment for yourself-sake

Love Yourself Aromatherapy

•

•

-
-

Loving oneself is one of the essences of a healthy being, along with the choices we make, if you are feeling a little down, Try smelling the aroma of something beautiful to uplift your mood! such as your favorite perfume, flower, scented oil, or a favorite scented candle.
If you have allergies, try a few deep breathing exercises, and yoga, consume foods rich in vitamin D and Consult your healthcare provider if you are depressed, for more options for balancing your mental and physical being.
Written by Anita Johnson-Brown

Look at me I am unique and special
Every human being on the earth is special, with their unique style, no matter who you are. The flaws you bear are a part of your identity, they bring out the beauty and magnificence of you. Look in the mirror and sample the pleasures of your vision of yourself. At that moment you accepted the one and only you.
Written by Anita Johnson-Brown

Anita Brown's Commentary: Hope for Tomorrow

-
-
-
-

There is a vision of Hope when you see the sun peeking out from the clouds, that bright cast of light is reason to believe there are better days to come.

Written by Anita Johnson-Brown

Anita Brown's Commentary: Spiritual

-
-
-
-

1. In the mist and of dark clouds, there is a small glow of light like that of the eye of a needle, it is an impending realm of hope.
2. Cast your eyes upon those you desire to trust, the realm of trust; should not be given freely. Trust not, until Trust has been earned.
3. A lesson learned is a gift of Wisdom.
4. Living by the word of The Heavenly Father and Jesus Christ, morals, and respect is an avenue that leads to faith and courage, and knowledge about life. And while I am a spiritual woman, you have the right to choose your way of life.

Written by Anita Johnson-Brown

Anita Brown's Commentary-Facts

-
-
-
-

This commentary is a fact!

When faced with multiple negative situations, placed upon you by others, and it seems impossible to move forward, do not submit to vengeance, and overwhelming thoughts of hatred, find peace of mind, by quietly venting, and allowing forgiveness, and

remember what comes out of the mouth defiles the spirit and hurts others.
I never believed the saying; words do not hurt! Words cause wars, emotional distress, heartache, embarrassment, and sometimes loss of life. Words are weapons, Good or Bad, and the words we say can set someone free or bond them for life.
When and if you must vent sometime a good scream in an isolated area might do the trick.

Prayers
Romans 12:19 KJV: Dearly beloved, avenge not yourselves, but rather give place unto wrath: for it is written, Vengeance is mine; I will repay, saith the Lord.
Romans 12:19, NASB: Never take your revenge, beloved, but leave room for the wrath of God, for it is written: 'VENGEANCE IS MINE, I WILL REPAY,' says the Lord.
Quoted from the Bible

It is important not to come out of character due to unfair, demeaning acts against you committed by others, they shall reap their rewards!
(AJ-B) Written by Anita Johnson-Brown

Anita Brown's Commentary: Elders

•

•

•

•

The art of wisdom and growing older
The transformation into maturity comes with aging and allowing the beauty marks of growing older to show their artistry, of the

gift of Wisdom. Elder people have strong intuition, they have battled the trials of life and deserve to be respected, they have borne the troubles of yesteryear to open doors for you to enter seed, flourish and be successful.
Written by Anita Johnson-Brown

All About Love

My Rose of Desire is an expression of Love and petals of pleasure. This is how we make each other feel.

To Anita: My Honey Love

A burning rose of desire is the way you light my fire, it ignites my burning flame to a forever-lasting passion only for you. Your touch and vibe ignite my soul and makes me drip like candle wax, so warm and soft, the liquid pours down your breast and trickles around your belly button, I take in a whiff of your perfume, and it cascades in my memory of my rose of desire.

I wish to taste her secret, and she desires to manipulate mine, gentle strokes of desire and rose petals float inside her ocean of love as we lay submerged in our passion, she lights every inch of my love wand, and the softness of her voice whispers in my ear and I begin to melt from the heat of her delicate touch. Her hands wander over my body to explore every inch of sensual weakness, she seduces and satisfies me. She delights in the loyal pleasures of craving only me, and I fill her rose pedal with every inch of me. My sweet rose of desire touches my ear with the most intimate touch of gentle aggression and whispers, "love more" She is mine, my pretty gorgeous, lovely, curvy, rose of desire, pleasing and immersing me with waves of intimate opulence, the only love I desire.

To Chris: My Baby Love
I am captivated by your mind, body, and soul, with love, as I slowly sip, drinking your love potion, hypnotized by the tiny beads of sweat dripping from his body.
Spellbinding me as we gaze at the red moon, together we want in a timeless capsule of love with each other while gliding on a pillow of softness as one, mentally and physically, with no thoughts of anyone during these moments. I long to curb his appetite and without distractions, when we are alone, he shows me the elements of ideal love, as we commit to fulfilling each other's every need. I am his oxygen, and he is my air, we are each other's heart's desire, and from his heart to my heart our love beads lather and pour like soft drops of rain, Drops of my morning dew fall against his moist skin and it smells so sweet as it penetrates my nostrils, and carries me into a deeper trance of pure seduction.

For Anita:
Your gentle and smooth touch put me in a pleasureful daze, and your caramel skin is a beauty to gaze upon, the body is plush and lovely, and my strong heart weakens as she overdoses me with her love and liquid honey. I cannot get enough of her, and she cannot enough of me, she begs for all of me. She has become my need to thrive, and I am her need to survive.

We are not shallow or dense, we are a knot of love for one another, we are God's Plan of two loves combined as one, just as the stars are seated in the sky and the moon shines its light at night. The sun rises and lights our way in the day and the beauty of the sunset gave us the notion to plunge into matrimony as a promise of our everlasting Love.

Our Promise:
Like the petals of a flower, I will catch you when you fall, I will gather the branches and twigs to build you an eternity, just as there is a heaven and earth, we will make a language of love and melodies, flowing expressively of the love we feel. You light the torch of my desire, and guide me into a lifetime of brightness, it amazes me how we convey our love. Our thoughts find a way to each of us when we are away from each other, It is as if the third eye of vision travels to unite us.
Like nature intended we come together like a blooming rose. We will always share an explosive love while spreading petals of desire and indulging the angelic smell of roses. Our Precious desires and thoughts are no longer just a dream they are our reality, My Rose of Desire.

Written by Anita Johnson-Brown and Christopher Maurice Brown

Anita Brown's Commentary: The waking of life, nature, and balance

•

•

•

•

Sometimes you need to step outside into the rain, to hear water falling, and hear the distant wind blowing when the breeze blows across your face, it is a reminder of new things to come.
in other words, sometimes your need to step out into the rain to appreciate the sunshine and see the flowers blooming. Everything has a purpose, a destiny, and a balance until we disturb its Homeostasis, mentally physically, and geographically.
Written by Anita Johnson-Brown

Anita Brown's Commentary: Know your Friends

•

•

•

•

There is an old saying that my parents taught me, two heads are better than one! unless the other head has undermined, has thoughts of sabotage, and plans to be deceitful, and manipulating. Choose your friends, business associates, and intimate partners with much thought!

Written by Anita Johnson-Brown

Anita Brown's Commentary-Perfection

-
-
-
-

There is no such thing as a perfect human being or perfect works, perfection is beyond our reach, your works may sound good, look good, and feel great, but to say they are perfect is a means to satisfy our needs, to be great at what we do.
Show me something you conceive to be perfect, and I will show you a human being who has the spiritual realm of the entirety gift of wisdom and remember this is my opinion.
There is also no such thing as perfection when it comes to love, true love is free, blissful, and has an urgent need to be satisfied, and can cause a multitude of emotions, heartache, joy, and a feeling of being safe and warm. Intimate relationships must be worked on to survive in this world of tempting pleasures.

Written by Anita Johnson-Brown

Anita Brown's Commentary: Trust

-
-
-
-

Socialize with people you can trust, depend on, and who have a radiance of platonic love, and may you extend the same blessings upon them.
Written by Anita Johnson-Brown

A stab in the back is a source of hatred, jealousy, envy, and a lack of maturity. Extend the gift of good nature, and love, and exclude yourself from others who show you a lack of affection and who are unwilling to be there for you when you need them, each person is as important as the other.

Written by Anita Johnson-Brown

Anita Johnson-Brown

Anita Brown's Commentary-Words that count.

-
-

-
-

A man is not a man of his word until he keeps it. Words can be expressed in many ways, by methods of writing, gestures, body language, and spoken verbally.

Written by Anita Johnson-Brown

Anita Brown's Commentary: Fun and Responsible

-
-
-
-

Life is better when you enjoy it, live your life to the fullest, but responsible, and know that your life is important to others just as it is to you. Be wise about the choices you make and the people you allow to enter your world, surround yourself with good people, and avoid the demanding shortcuts of temptations, which lead to disastrous situations. Hurting yourself or letting others hurt you physically, or emotionally, has an impact on the people who care about you.

Anita Johnson-Brown, Editor

Anita Brown's Commentary-Not another round

-
-

-
-

1. To be one with another you must have a mental connection, and to be honest I must be physically attracted to you.
2. Intimately speaking, never return to the ex that caused you to lose your spirit, by changing your character from good to bad, stirring up anger within your heart, and soul, or subjecting you to any type of abuse. Think about why you broke up with this person. When I see an ex-, I wonder how I ever let them in my life, if I encountered an ex-who made my life a living nightmare, or anyone I dated previously, I would greet them be kind, then avoid them like the plague. My advice is do not do exes, the merry-go-round of heck does not fit into my schedule, but if you are adjusted to that type of ride, Enjoy!
3. Forgiveness is important, although it is hard to forget. Forgiving someone does not mean you need to associate with them, if they caused stress, discomfort, or fear and forced you to the perils of negative energy, relieve yourself of their presence.
4. If you cannot keep a secret, I cannot trust you!
5. Get to Know someone completely before you give them all your love.

Written by Anita Johnson-Brown

Anita Brown's Commentary: The balance of human and earth

-
-
-
-

The human body has an immune system that is designed to fight germs, just as the earth was created to fight back for its survival, and for the survival of humans, creatures, plants, insects, animals, etc., every living thing has a purpose. What we destroy, destroys

us!
Written by Anita Johnson-Brown

Tid-Bits and Tallywags
Let us break for a riddle. Hop on the Tid-Bit and Tallywags brain Teaser, and Figure this one out!
I hope your next borborygmus does not lead to collywobbles!
Written by Anita Johnson-Brown

More of Anita Brown's Commentary

Anita Brown's Commentary: Friends Only

•

•

•

•

Sprinkle Platonic Love:
Everyone needs to know there is a caring person in the world, smile at a co-worker, relatives, neighbor, and friends.
Be kind caring, courteous, and considerate, platonic love is different from intimate attraction, friendships, and love relationships, respect the word no and what it means.
Written by Anita Johnson-Brown

Anita Brown's Commentary: Unfold the Mystery

•

•

•

•

I am like a book of sweet mysteries, to get to know me, you must unfold the mystery in me.
Written by Anita Johnson-Brown

Anita Brown's Commentary: The Downner

•

•

•

•

Commit yourself not to be a part of someone else's misery, and deal with your emotions, so you will be an uplifting friend, good intimate partner, relative, co-worker, etc.
People should be excited and thrilled to be in your presence, and not look upon you as a troublemaker, backstabber, or a miserable person, who sheds darkness on the realm of light.
Leave an impression of goodness.
Written by Anita Johnson-Brown

Anita Brown's Commentary: The symbol of Love

•

•

•

•

When given an engagement ring, be happy you were chosen to be a man's wife or a woman's husband, it is not the size of the ring that counts, the number of carats, the price, or whether it is yellow or white gold, silver, or Platinum because LOVE is priceless.
Written by Anita Johnson-Brown

Anita Brown's Commentary: Wake me up Now!

-
-
-
-

What you see is not always what you get, all that glitters may end up tarnishing.
The man with the best hand has wisdom and looks beyond outside beauty and ends up with a gem for life.
You cannot complain about something you said you bought but did not pay for it.
Written by Anita Johnson-Brown

Anita Brown's Commentary: Screw the BS

•

•

•

•

Here is a question that remains unanswered
Why would a person be diagnosed with a personality disorder because they refused to put up with another person's demeaning behavior, and verbal abuse?
Written by Anita Johnson-Brown

Anita Brown's Commentary: Kind, Fierce, and strong

•

•

•

•

Be courteous but courageous, in any of your endeavors.
Written by Anita Johnson-Brown

Anita Brown's Commentary: Be Wise

-
-
-
-

A wise old man once told me, never give anyone all you have, because you will end up wishing in one hand and Shittin in the other one.

A wise woman once told me, to be good to others you must first be good to yourself!

From the mouths of wisdom and parenting.

Written by Anita Johnson-Brown

Anita Brown's Commentary: Bad thoughts go away

-
-
-
-

Pillows are symbols of relaxation, a frowning face is a symbol of dislike, and maybe hate, a smirk is a symbol of jealousy, envy, or a mistake, and a doorway to misery, so while you are resting on the pillow of rest, forget about the mistake, you made, thoughts

of jealousy and misery, these feeling set the emotions rolling for a downfall. Learn to forgive yourself.
Written by Anita Johnson-Brown

Anita Brown's Commentary: Teach me

•
•
•
•

Here is a word of advice, teach your children to pray! read to them and be a role model, children need parents they can look to for guidance and inspiration.

Written by Anita Johnson-Brown

Anita Brown's Commentary-Growth and respect

•
•
•
•

What you instruct your children today will follow them for the rest of their lives, be mindful of what your body language says, and the verbiage spoken around children.
Written by Anita Johnson-Brown

Anita Brown's Commentary: Mindsets

•

•

•

•

Trust tips and Mindsets

1. if you must go through your partner's phone, wallet, or other personal belongings without permission, there is a trust issue that must be addressed. Think About it!
2. One size never fits all every person; each natural body has its unique shape. Trust me on this one.
3. Adults, no matter how old you are! never be afraid to Love, make behavior changes, live life to the fullest responsibly, or hold yourself back from achieving a goal on which you have been working.
4. Alone time is good for mental and physical rejuvenation.

Written by Anita Johnson-Brown

Anita Brown's Commentary: straight to the Point

•

•

•

•

The A.B.C.'s

It is better to have two left shoes, than no shoes at all, get creative and use one of the shoes to design one for the right foot.

Written by Anita Johnson-Brown

Anita Brown's Commentary- My sayings!

•

•

•

•

1. If you do not have anything nice to say, do not say anything at all, a wise man keeps his mouth shut when trouble is stirring and moves away swiftly.
2. It is easier to burn friendships than calories.
3. Take care of your business before basking in pleasure.
4. Pure beauty has imperfect imperfections.
5. When you are confused or in doubt about a specific situation, keep it professional and just say, Dats-one-ah- dem-dare-thangs, a reminder of riddles and slang. Be polite, smile, and walk away because you can recognize a fib a mile away. Relax and consider options on how to manage the situation another day.

Thank you for reading Anita Brown's Commentary,
written by Anita Johnson-Brown.

Anita Brown's Commentary: Matters of the Heart

•

•

•

•

Matters of the Heart

1. Time heals mental and physical setbacks as well as helping mend broken hearts, but the memories last a lifetime.
2. Time limits are just as important as time extensions. One amount of time is less than the other.
3. Some say Power is greater than love, However, Love allowed you to gain the knowledge to receive Power. Think about it, knowledge is power, and riches allow you to have power, but you cannot buy the power of love. You can buy the company of someone to soothe your urges for love, and the one you love without love in return.
4. The one who loves you does not care about million-dollar bank accounts, they have the wisdom of mustard seed, needle knowledge, and if you do not! pick up a copy of the book of life.
Financial survival is necessary, but money greed is the root of iniquity.
5. Greater is the love that reciprocates your attention.
6. Let no words of evil or backstabbing word be the sour taste in your speech, it is best to reframe from those who cause you to lose your character and drain your spirit.
7. Sow seeds that bloom, not wither and die when your presence is known, in other words... when you enter a room or your name is heard, may the crowd cheer and not say "oh no it's you again!
8. False love is a road to unhappiness and intimate hell; it is just as bad as learning to love someone you are not the least bit attracted to.
9. There's nothing like being with someone who makes you feel safe, loved, and needed, and makes your body send signals of undying desire.
10. No matter what gender, age, the mental or physical condition we are in, Love has the power to develop a passion for intimacy.
11. Human beings need love and understanding.
Written by Anita Johnson-Brown-Editor

Anita Brown's Commentary: Prayer and children

•

•

•

•

Parents, teach your children to pray, be patient, and make decisions based on facts and reframe from being hasty in matters of anger and frustration.
Written by Anita Johnson-Brown

Anita Brown's Commentary-The Heart

•

•

•

•

Sometimes the heart speaks louder than words, but human beings need to hear the words "I LOVE YOU", it is not a want, it is a need!
By Anita Johnson-Brown
People need to know they are loved and appreciated.
Written by Anita Johnson-Brown

Anita Brown's Commentary: You Are Somebody

•

•

•

•

When you have been cast to the side as nobody, remember you are somebody, created in the uniqueness of God's image.
Written by Anita Johnson-Brown

•

•

•

•

•

•

• Anita Brown's Commentary
Love vs Friends
Be Kind, Caring, and loving, and never mistake platonic

relationships as the gateway to intimacy, unless there is an intimate connection. Some gifts and acts of kindness and someone cares about you.
With Love
written by Anita Johnson-Brown

Anita Brown's Commentary: Good News

•

•

•

•

Good News Never Grow Old! These memories and stories become part of our history. Share your Good News.
written by Anita Johnson-Brown

Anita Brown's Commentary: Never Give Up!

•

•

•

•

The heart is so well designed and submits itself to broken hearts, shattered dreams, thoughts of dreams, and fantasies, and most of all it is designed to accept reality, never give up, and be creative. Yesterday is yesterday and tomorrow is tomorrow, and who knows with God's Blessing your tomorrow may come today, and if not today, soon, never give up.
Written by CBAJ-B

Anita Brown's Commentary: Learning every Day

•

•

•

•

It does not matter what I know in a manner of speaking, what matters is what I need to Learn.

Written by Anita Johnson-Brown

Anita Brown's Commentary: The Facts Please

-
-
-
-

Messages that are short, and straight to the point, help to summarize the facts, after researching the truth. (We call this the nitty gritty) as my mom used to say.
Written by Anita Johnson-Brown

Anita Brown's Commentary: The passion of Man and Woman

-
-
-
-

Speaking about relationships, and love, being with someone that keeps you feeling youthful, lifts you, has your back, and gives you the spirit of energy to push through inconvenient situations is a joy to be with.

A person who sends waves of electronic passion up and down your body when you look at them and makes your body tingle with desire, keeps the ingredients of chemistry flowing.
. Written by Anita Johnson-Brown

Anita Brown's Commentary: your opinions matter

•

•

•

•

Your opinions matter, they are Important factors in the things we believe in on a discovery of what matters most, and the bloodline to Debates.
Thank you for reading Anita Brown's Commentary
Written by Anita Johnson-Brown

Anita Brown's Commentary

•

•

•

•

Blessed is many, but so few are thankful!
Written by Anita Johnson-Brown

Anita Brown's Commentary: Knowledge

•

•

•

•

Grow and learn from your mistakes and experiences, the knowledge you have learned over the years is wisdom, which should be shared with the younger generation.

Knowing something is better than knowing nothing.
If it is true that time waits for no one, what are you waiting for? it is never too late, one day a door will open that man will never have the power to close.
The path to success is the determination to succeed.
Written by Anita Johnson-Brown, Editor

Anita Brown's Commentary: Thank You

•

•

•

•

Without expressing thanks to someone, they assume they are not appreciated.
Written by Anita Johnson-Brown

Anita Brown's Commentary: Darkness to Light

•

•

•

•

In the waking hour of anxiety and madness, anger rises and will pass, just as the leaves fall to the ground, so shall better days come when bitterness is just a mist in the wind, in a matter of time as the Seasons change.
Parables, written by Anita Johnson-Brown, Editor

Anita Brown's Commentary: Children

•

•

•

•

Children are a blessing, let us treat them that way while showing them love, teaching them responsibility, morals, respect, and dignity, and counting each mistake as a learning experience. Disciplining a child should not be conducted in an abusive manner. Teach your child to be open to every culture without prejudice and gain as much knowledge as possible in a multitude of subjects and pray for wisdom.
Written by Anita Johnson-Brown

Anita Brown's Commentary: The facts of the A's & B's
(A) Broken Promises are an explanation of Broken Trust! and a journey on the trail of goodbyes. Losing friendships over lies and deceit shows a lack of trust and intelligence.
(B) Being yourself exuberates a unique and extraordinary human being!
Written by Anita Johnson-Brown

Anita Brown's Commentary: Support and Caring

•

•

•

•

When friends, family, and known associates won't support your endeavors to make goals come true! someone else will, however, wooden nickels are never free, and as our parents once said "don't accept any wooden nickels", or sign contracts that have not been read, and beware of stranger baring gifts, his smile looks genuine, but his intentions are deadly" If the gifts he brings are of good deeds, he will not accept anything in return, for his revenue is the thrill of seeing you succeed.

Written by Anita Johnson-Brown

Anita Brown's Commentary: Self-Love

•

•

•

•

If you have the notion that Love has passed you by, look in the mirror, self-love comes first.
Love you, and Intimate Love will follow!
With love
Written by Anita Johnson-Brown

Anita Brown's Commentary: New Things

Open your world to new adventures, and live life to the fullest, something special may be waiting for you on the other side of destiny!
Written by Anita Johnson-Brown

Anita Brown's Commentary: Parents

If you are blessed enough to have your parents, and they have not passed through to the gates of Heaven or elsewhere, and your parents are good people, listen to what they have to say. I promise that constructive criticism, a little tough love, morals and standards, and respect for others, go a long way.
It takes more than money, fast cars, rich friends, and a boat full of people, to be an adult!
Remember wisdom is gained through experience and the words spoken and taught by elders. A person without wisdom is lacking

intelligence.
Words from the horse's mouth, speak the truth! It is a riddle and a blessing!
If someone was not taught or learned improper behavior, who should be blamed? I know, do you?

Written by Anita Johnson-Brown

Anita Brown's Commentary: Goals

-
-
-
-

No matter how hard someone or something tries to knock you down, never give up! The obstacles may be a sign of caution, a detour away from danger, or an obstacle pushing you toward another entrance to success.
Putting forth a little effort each day is an attempt to reach your most impossible dreams.
If something sounds too good to be true, well you know the saying! Work hard to get what you want, and do it legally, respectfully, and honestly! without harming others.
Written by Anita Johnson-Brown

Anita Brown's Commentary: Be good to You

If you step out into the coldness of winter, you will get cold, and feel your body temperature drop and ripple down to your bones,

so you dawn yourself in warm attire to protect your body which is a normal action.
On another note, while protecting your body, protect your mind as well! mental thriving is also essential to good health! Do not allow the coldness of the chilling hands of a mental abuser, to steal your joy, Guard yourself against those who penetrate your body, mind, and soul with bad deeds of rage.

You cannot challenge mother nature, and you absolutely cannot pass the hands of father time without harming yourself or others.
Written by Anita Johnson-Brown

Teach yourself to be confident in all that you do, and in all you do, do it with love.
Suttle words and put-downs, from strangers and friends, allow you to subtract them from your life and open you up to the realization that they are minus of the plus signs that equal a well-balanced life.

Thank you for reading Anita Brown's Commentary, written, and created by Anita Johnson-Brown, book 2 coming soon!
Anita Brown's Commentary—Anita Brown's Commentary is my opinion, about the facts and other subjects of matter, and the words written are not meant to persuade how you choose to live. Or think.

Get to know Anita Johnson-Brown and owner of The Los Angeles News digital
Newspaper. Los Angeles News losangelesnews.town.news/

Connect with me via email at anitajb@authoranitajohnsonbrown.com
And on social media Search, Anita Johnson-Brown

www.ingramcontent.com/pod-product-compliance
Lightning Source LLC
LaVergne TN
LVHW052106160826
845678LV00015B/3400